# More Jokes, Riddles and Scenarios for Happy Kids

By

Myles O'Smiles

### Cataloguing in Publication Data

Myles O'Smiles

More Jokes, Riddles and Scenarios for Happy Kids

Description: Crimson Hill Books trade paperback edition | Nova Scotia, Canada

ISBN 978-1-988650-68-5 (Paperback)

BISAC: JNF028020 Juvenile Nonfiction: Humor - Jokes & Riddles | JNF021050 Juvenile Nonfiction: Games & Activities - Questions & Answers | JNF021070 Juvenile Nonfiction: Games & Activities - Word Games

THEMA: Y - Children's, Teenage & Educational | YPC - Educational: Language, literature & literacy | YNU - Children's / Teenage general interest: Humour & jokes

Record available at https://www.bac-lac.gc.ca/eng/Pages/home.aspx

Illustrations: Camilo Luis Berneri
Book design and formatting: Jesse Johnson

Crimson Hill Books
(a division of)
Crimson Hill Products Inc.
Wolfville, Nova Scotia
Canada

MORE FUN JOKES, RIDDLES AND SCENARIOS FOR HAPPY KIDS is a children's word game book. It has lots of funny jokes, what-if and would-you-rather scenarios and tricky riddle questions to entertain and delight kids plus hilarious cartoon illustrations.

Readers ages 8 to 12 and older will enjoy these jokes, scenarios and riddles, both reading them and sharing them with family and friends.

These word games are a fun way to improve reading, problem-solving, communication and social skills for young readers, new readers, ESL students and anyone who likes to play with language!

Everything in this book is a kid-pleaser and family-friendly! Hours of fun for everyone!

## Having Fun with Jokes, Riddles and Scenarios

Hey, want to hear some funny jokes and clever riddles? You'll find lots of them in this book!

There are also plenty of fun scenarios. A scenario is a word picture of something that is happening or could happen. You could also call it a situation, or a story-starter. Scenarios ask, "What if…?" or "Would you rather?" questions.

Every day you're in a lot of scenarios! When you think about what you want to do on the weekend or what kind of party you want to celebrate your next birthday, you're creating scenarios in your head. You're imagining what would be the most wonderful time you could share with your family and friends!

So, put on your thinking antlers for these fun and silly jokes, awesome riddles and clever scenarios!

Turn the page and let's get this word party started!

Myles O'Smiles

## Jokes

**1.** People who like to gossip have this. What is it?
*A great sense of rumor.*

**2.** Time flies like an eagle. How does fruit fly?
*Fruit flies like a banana.*

**3.** How do billboards talk?
*They use sign language.*

**4.** What time is it when you're having fun jumping on your trampoline?
*Spring-time!*

**5.** What's the shortest birthday you'll ever have in your life?
*Your thirty-second birthday.*

**6.** What's the difference between a cat and a comma?
*A cat has claws at the end of her paws, and a comma marks a pause at the end of a clause.*

**7.** Where do you go to learn how to make ice cream?
*Sundae school.*

**8.** Why did Lettuce win the race against Tomato?
*Lettuce was a head and tomato was trying to ketchup.*

**9.** What do you call a chicken when they're crossing the road?
*Poultry in motion.*

**10.** What did the lamp say when it was turned off?
*"I'm delighted!"*

**11.** *Roses are red,*
*Here's something new.*
*Violets are violet,*
*They're never blue.*
*Anyone who says so*
*has been lying to you!*

**12.** Why did the girl say she was good friends with 25 letters of the alphabet?
*She didn't know "Y."*

**13.** What do you call a short fortune-teller who escapes from prison?
*A small medium at large.*

**14.** What do firefighters like to put in their soup?
*Fire-crackers.*

**15.** The dictionary goes from "A" to "Z."But what goes from "Z" to "A?"
*A zebra.*

**16.** *Knock, knock.*
*Who's there?*
*Atch.*
*Atch who?*
*Sorry, I didn't know you had a cold.*

**17.** What are Daisy the cow's favorite magazines?
*She really enjoys reading cattle-logs.*

**18.** *Knock, knock.*
*Who's there?*
*Yodel-lay-he.*
*Yodel-lay-he-who?*
*I didn't know you could yodel!*

**19.** *Knock, knock.*
*Who's there?*
*Goat.*

*Goat who?*
*Goat to the door and find out.*

**20.** *Knock, knock.*
*Who's there?*
*Justin.*
*Justin who?*
*Justin time for dinner!*

**21.** There is only one Disney™ character who has a middle name. Who is it?

*Donald Duck, whose full name is Donald Fauntleroy Duck. Fauntleroy (or faunt le roi) is French for "Defend the King!"*

**22.** One…two…three…four…five…six…seven…eight. What is true of all these numbers, when you spell them out in English?
*None of these numbers has the letter "A" in it.*

**23.** If you wrote out numbers, starting with one…two…three…how many numbers would you need to write down before you'd get to a number that DOES have the letter "A" in it?
*1,000. You'd get all the way up to 999 without EVER writing an "A" in these numbers' names.*

**24.** How do ranchers count their cattle?
*With a cow-culator.*

**25.** *Knock, knock.*
*Who's there?*
*Amos.*
*Amos who?*
*A mosquito!*

**26.** *There once was a farmer from Leeds*
*who swallowed a packet of seeds.*
*It soon came to pass*
*he was covered with grass.*
*But he has all the tomatoes he needs!*

**27.** *I'd rather have fingers than toes,*
*I'd rather have ears than a nose.*
*And as for my hair,*
*I'm glad it's all there,*
*I'd be awfully sad, if it goes.*

**28.** *There was an old man of Broadheath*
*Who sat on his set of false teeth.*
*He cried out, in pain,*
*"I've done it again!*
*"I've bitten myself – underneath!"*

**29.** *There once was a fly on the wall,*
*I wonder why it didn't fall?*
*Because its feet stuck?*
*Or was it just luck?*
*Or does gravity miss things that small?*

**30.** *Amazingly, green seaweed stew,*
*Is supposed to be better for you*
*than a pie of baked rat.*
*It's because of the fat.*
*But I guess that you already knew.*

**31.** *There was an odd man in Peru*
*Who dreamt he was eating his shoe.*
*He awoke with a fright*
*In the middle of the night*
*And found out his dream had come true!*

**32.** *The teacher said, "Class, listen to this!"*
*"Said backward, your name has a twist!"*
*One kid caught her eye.*
*She said, "Simon, why don't you try?"*
*He thought for a moment, then said, "No, mis!"*

**33.** *There once was a woman from Chester,*
*Whose knowledge grew lesser and lesser.*
*It at last grew so small,*
*She knew nearly nothing at all,*
*And now she's a college professor.*

**34.** *Written with a pen, sealed with a kiss,*
*If you're my friend, can you answer me this:*

*Are we friends, or are we not?*
*You told me once, but I forgot.*

*Please tell me now, and tell me true,*
*I want to say I'm best friends with you.*

*Of all the kids I've ever met,*
*You're the one I'll never forget.*

*There isn't a thing I wouldn't do,*
*To have a friend who's just like you!*

**35.** How do you make varnish disappear?
*You take out the "r."*

**36.** If you keep walking on a straight path, how far can you walk into a forest?
*Only halfway. After that, you're walking out of the forest.*

**37.** How many balls of string would it take to reach the moon?
*One, if it were a big enough ball of string.*

**38.** What do you call a very popular perfume?
*A best smeller.*

**39.** What is a regretful witch doctor's mistake?
*A voodoo boo-hoo boo-boo.*

**40.** What did the police officer give the noisy dog's owner?
*A barking ticket.*

**41.** What kind of bees can never make up their minds?
*May-bees.*

**42.** What do you call a REALLY big ant?
*A gi-ANT.*

**43.** What is the difference between a fake $10 bill (or £10 note) and an angry rabbit?
*One is bad money; the other is a mad bunny.*

## Riddles

**1.** Where did the geologists go on a date?

*To a rock concert.*

**2.** What did the mother cat need when she wanted to take a quiet nap?

*A kitty-sitter.*

**3.** What kind of beds do mermaids sleep in?

*Water beds.*

**4.** What does this mean – AHIBVE

*Bee in a hive.*

**5.** What does this mean – VAD   ERS

*Space invaders.*

**6.** I build my house brand new each year.
Taking care no humans are near.
My home is open to the sky.
To reach it, you might need to fly.
When they get too big, my babies leave.
Careless squirrels are my biggest peeve.

Give me seeds and I will sing,
Another summer day my song will bring.
And here's another clue for you all
You can tell my name when you hear my call.

What am I?

*A songbird. Some songbirds you might know: robins, sparrows, finches, chickadees, cardinals, towhee, wrens, blackbirds, jays and orioles.*

*Fun Fact: There are more than 5,000 known types of songbirds in the world!*

**7.** First, you put everything you own in boxes, or wrap them up and put them in a car or truck.
Then you drive somewhere.
Then you unpack all those boxes and put everything you own away where it belongs.

What are you doing?

*Moving to a new home.*

**8.** I glow in the dark but remain dark most days.
Always ready, awaiting the time when you need me.
Waiting for times when you work, or you play.
Your desk is where I'll always be.
Waiting to shine, whenever you say.

Just flick my switch and I'll light up your life.
I'm ready to serve any dull day or night!

What am I?

*Your desk lamp.*

9. Put my head to the page,
   My cap at my feet,
   I light up the words
   That you want to keep.
   If you own a book, you can use me.
   If the book's not yours, you must refuse me.

   What am I?

   *A highlighter.*

10. I can be any colour you could name.
    I'm tall and skinny; drawing things is my game.
    I'm fun to own and fun to use,
    But sometimes just so easy to lose.
    Take care of me and I'll always be,
    Ready to create when you uncap me!

    What am I?

    *A coloured marker pen (or liquid crayon).*

**11.** When I'm a baby I've got feathery fur.
When I'm happy, I'll sit on your lap and purr.
I love to jump, but also to sleep,
Give me a safe home, it's your kindness I seek.

Fresh water, fresh food, a soft pillow or bed
Just these, plus kindness, are all that I need.
To be your sweet companion,
Means the world to me.

Who am I?

*Your pet cat.*

**12.** Endless white, with pale lines,
Inviting you to try some rhymes.
Or maybe notes, thoughts, or ideas
Or anything your heart desires.
You use me often and fill me up.
But without a pen, pencil or crayon,
I remain nothing but space and lines.

What am I?

*A pad of lined paper or a journal notebook.*

**13.** Some people like to unbend me.
Some bend me back, thinking they'll mend me.
Some join me to paper, my true ambition.
Keeping pages together is my life's work and
mission.

What am I?

*A paper-clip.*

**14.** Do you read books under the covers?
Is this your secret bedtime delight?
Or your passion is reading late into the night?
But no one must know! So, don't turn on a light!

Reach for me instead; no lights you'll need!
It could be you're travelling, near or abroad.
Just one book in your pocket

Won't be nearly enough!

Once again I will serve you, at home or away.
Your constant companion, both night and day.

What am I?

*Your e-reader or any wireless electronic device that allows you to read books, such as a tablet or smart phone.*

15. I open my mouth to swallow your files.
I close my mouth to hide them away.
I open my mouth to help you search.
I close my mouth to keep what you find safe.

What am I?

*A file cabinet.*

16. You sit over me to work or play.
This could be at night, it could be every day.
On my back I might carry a confusion of things,
Might start off neat and end up messy.

I'm made of wood, plastic, metal or glass.
I've been used since ancient times, with few changes.
Every famous person throughout the ages has had at least one of me.

What am I?

*A desk.*

17. I bloom where I'm planted.
    Grow where I'm placed.
    I live in homes big and small.
    I don't take up much space.

    My few needs are simple;
    water, air and sunshine.
    Give me these, and some warmth,
    A true gift I will make.

    What am I?

    *A houseplant.*

18. I have legs but no back.
    A body, but no head.
    You might sit on me, or stand on me,
    I might hold a book or a lamp near your bed.
    I can be any colour, and usually made of wood.
    Or plastic, or metal.
    I'm always ready to when you want to rest.

    What am I?

    *A bench or stool.*

**19.** What happened to Mr. Frog's car when it broke down?

*It got toad away.*

**20.** You might call me old-fashioned,
As many modern people do.
Yet every car has me
Many homes have me too,
Though not many schools.
I can tell you the news,
Or play you some tunes.
Or I might tell you stories.
Making pictures with sound.

What am I?

*A radio.*

**21.** In winter I'm green.
In summer I'm green.
And in spring. And in fall.
While others show their skeletons to the sky,
I am unchanging, always dressed modestly.
Strong at my centre. Slender at my tips,
Sometimes tall, slow to grow,
With deep roots, but always reaching to the sky.

What am I?

*An evergreen tree. Some types of evergreens you might know of are pine, spruce, hemlock, yew, cypress, fir, tamarack and cedar.*

*Where you live, there might also be other types of evergreens growing, such as eucalyptus and magnolia. Most rainforest trees are also evergreen.*

*There are also some evergreen shrubs that answer this riddle, such as holly and rhododendron.*

*Fun Fact: Evergreen trees and shrubs grow on every continent except Antarctica.*

**22.** Can you spot something unusual about these 12 words? They are:
ahoy, blow, chin, defy, erst, flux, gist, hint, imps, know, lops and most.

Once you have the answer, do you know a 5-letter word that does the same thing? There's also a 6-letter word with this unusual trait.

Do you know what they are?

*These 12 words are all 4-letter words, but that's not the answer. The letters in each of these special words are in alphabetical order.*
*This is also true for these 2 words: below and almost.*

**23.** A farmer who plants hundreds of _ _ _ _ _ of grains every year _ _ _ _ _ deeply about the amount of rainfall. When there isn't enough rain, he _ _ _ _ _ around with his watering equipment because it's dry enough to _ _ _ _ _ him about the possibility of his crops failing.

Each blank is a five-letter word made with these letters: AECRS.
Can you fill in the blanks so these sentences make sense?

*A farmer who plants hundreds of acres of grains every year cares deeply about the amount of rainfall. When there isn't enough rain, he races around with his watering equipment because it's dry enough to scare him about the possibility of his crops failing.*

**24.** Rearrange each of these words to find the names of foods:

Dasla

Toh gods

Wandsich

Players

Sandiers

Assuages

Lareby

*They are: salad, hot dogs, sandwich, parsley, sardines, sausages and barley.*

**25.** Ache is one of the few words in English that has "he" in it. There are just 2 words in English that have "he" twice in the same word. What are these 2 words?

*Headache and heartache.*

**26.** Every room you have ever been in, including the room you are in now, is full of this. So is every outside space you have ever been in.

What is it?

*Air.*

**27.** For centuries I lie waiting,
rumbling deep underground,

while roiling and boiling.
Anticipating.
Announcing my actions with mumbling sounds.

Your scientists study me, as they gather
Scans, numbers and data
Hoping to warn humans
Of my next encounter.

When next I'll erupt,
They can't agree.
I might give you no warning
I might cause you to flee.

On the day I explode
Billowing black clouds to the skies
Raining hot ash and lava
Everywhere that's nearby.

Molten, I crawl
Down the street where you live.
Swallowing all I encounter
Faint warnings I give.

I burn all in my path,
Then cool to stone
Nature's powerful reminder
Earth changing and growing.

I once buried Pompei

In only one day.
I'm alive in Hawaii now
No forces of good
can keep me at bay.

What am I?

*A volcano and its lava flow.*

28. Rearrange these nonsense words to make the names of six sweet treats:

> Eip
> Keac
> Cie macer
> Laermac rocn
> Kmlihaseks
> Tepaun titlebr

*They are pie, cake, ice cream, caramel corn, milkshakes and peanut brittle.*

29. Red, round, plump and juicy,
You might think I'm veggie,
but truly I'm fruity.

What am I?

*A tomato.*

**30.** The rarest colour in nature,
The colour of some cat's eyes.
The colour of water, reflected.
On clear days, for this colour
look up to the skies!

What is this?

*The colour blue.*

**31.** Rearrange each of these words to find the names of six sports:

Logf
Netsin
Creocs
Lofobatl
Yoheck
Kalblesblta

*They are golf, tennis, soccer, football, hockey and basketball.*

**32.** On this day of playing pranks
Will I fool you?
Or will I be the one who's fooled
By your simple, silly game?

What is this?

*April Fool's Day, April 1st each year.*

**33.** Dads love this
Dogs do, too.
If they could have this every day,
They'd never stop thanking you!

It comes in a package from the store,
When you eat it, you'll probably want more!
Peel it off the paper and throw it in the pan
So easy to cook, almost anyone can!

What is it?

*Bacon.*

**34.** Kids can't wait for this to start,
It means they can stay up late, maybe long after dark!
Read more books, play more games, ride bikes in the park!
Take swim lessons, have picnics, play at the beach,
No teachers, no school for 8 blissful weeks!

What is this?

*Summer vacation.*

**35.** We're thankful for our dear friends' and family's health,
We're thankful for our good fortune and wealth.

We're thankful for healthy food, music and fun times.
We might even be thankful for this silly rhyme!

There's so much we can give our sincere thanks for,
Home comforts, good news, kind friends and much more!
No matter what comes our way, both today and tomorrow,
Goodness that's shared will chase away any sorrows.

What is this describing?

*An attitude of gratitude. This means being thankful for all that is good in your life. What are 5 things you are most thankful for in your life right now?*

**36.** How do you make one disappear?

*Add a "G" and it's gone!*

**37.** White flesh above.
Brown gills below.
Never moving,
in darkness I grow.

What am I?

*A mushroom.*

**38.** You use me from your head to your toes,
the more I work for you, the thinner I grow!

What am I?

*A bar of soap.*

**39.** I'm skinny and flat.
I live on your desk.
Mice like me.
I'll never slip, but I might fall.
Sometimes I have words,
Sometimes just one colour.
Or maybe a picture
That makes you smile!

What am I?

*A mouse-pad for your computer.*

**40.** You pass through me at the start;
I'll be there at the end.
That's when you will cross over,
And call me your new-found friend!

What am I?

*The finish line of a race (the starting line and the finish line are the same).*

**41.** You use us when you make up words,
With 26 to choose from.
This riddle's easy when you stop and think.
The answer is right in front of you!

What are we?

*Letters of the alphabet.*

**42.** It passes but you can't hear it.
Sometimes though, you may think you feel it.
You will have it. Then it's gone,
You might want to stop it, but it always moves on!
You could lose it, or gain it; perhaps fear it, or claim
it,
But it keeps rolling on, belonging to no one.

What is it?

*Time*

**43.** I have lots to say, but I never speak.
You might come inside, if facts and answers you
seek.
Or for bold quests and adventures both strange and
wild,
Or funny jokes and stories that cause you to smile!

Some use me for work, others for pleasure,

Sometimes I'm free, yet my value beyond measure.
I go where you go, though I'm not alive,
Without all who are like me, mankind can't possibly thrive!

What am I, and others like me?

*We are books.*

**44.** I have no voice, but I can sing
Or talk. Or squawk. Or make all kinds of sounds
About anything and everything.
But I'm always silent till I get plugged in.

I might live on your desk,
Or near your TV.
I could hang on the wall,
Or stand on the floor.

You could find me inside your electronics
Or outside in summer.
At home, work or school.
Anywhere that sound quality matters.

What am I?

*A pair of speakers.*

**45.** Hey, do you want to go out to play?
Have fun adventures, go for car rides or run on the beach?
Have you got any cake, any cookies or treats?
Well, it's time to share them, stop being a tease!

Where've you been? Who did you see?
Did you have a fun day?
I'm so glad to see you!
But you went without me!

But wait! Have you heard? I've learned a new trick!
I can dance, jump or roll over,
Just say the word!
What will we do now? I'll let you pick!

I don't like my collar. No, I don't want a leash!
But I'll wear them and act nice,

If we can go for a walk – or maybe to the beach?

Now you've come home from school
I've been waiting ALL day!

Would you please please please please say
I'm your best friend, and
it's time to play!

Who am I?

*Your pet dog.*

## Scenarios

### 1. WOULD YOU RATHER:

Design clothing...

OR

Design buildings?

Sew the clothing you design...

OR

Be on the construction crew for a building you designed?

Wear the clothing you designed...

OR

Live in the building you designed?

Sell the clothing you designed and created...

OR

Sell the buildings you designed and helped build?

### 2. WOULD YOU RATHER:

Be a tennis ball...

OR

A hockey stick?

Go to a party...

OR

Hang out with your friends?

Go to a ball-game...

OR
Go to a concert?

Do homework...
OR
Babysit?
Why?

## 3. WOULD YOU RATHER:

Time travel to the day you were born...
OR
To the day of your favorite birthday, before you were 10 years old...
OR
To your 18th birthday...
OR
To any day in your life that you choose to visit?
What day did you pick and why did you choose it?

## 4. WOULD YOU RATHER:

Be a dog...
OR
A cat?

Be a bird of prey...
OR
A songbird?

Be a flower...
OR

A tree?

Be a snake...
OR
A lizard?

Be a fish...
OR
A hummingbird?

Why?

## 5. WOULD YOU RATHER:

Have a famous brother or sister...
OR
Be the most famous person in your family?

Be known for your intelligence...
OR
Be known for your honesty?

Be known for your kindness...
OR
For how good you are at sports?

Be an inventor...
OR
Be an explorer?

Why?

**6. WOULD YOU RATHER:**

Be a professional soccer player...
OR
A professional figure skater...
OR
A professional skateboarder?

Live in a place where it snows for part of the year,
but summers are mild...
OR
Live in a place where it never snows, but summers
are very hot?

Play the bagpipes...
OR
Play the fiddle?

Spend your next vacation scuba diving...

OR
Shopping?

**7.** A relative you didn't even know you had leaves you a castle, complete with everything in it and all the land around it. This includes gardens, fields and even a village!

Describe your new castle and land. Where is it?

What does it look like?

What is it like to live there?

Who else lives there?

**8.** Unfortunately, your rich relative who left you the castle left all their money to somebody else.

Alas, the costs of running a castle are enormous. How will you pay the bills? Clearly, you need to make your new inheritance earn some money!

You might turn your castle into a luxury hotel. Or add a restaurant and gift shop, and charge tourists for house tours. Or rent your castle out for weddings and special events. Or rent out your castle or village as a setting for a movie.

Perhaps you'll do all these things? Or something else? You decide!

But you better be quick, because it is VERY expensive to run a castle AND you must pay all the people who work for you to keep it running!

9. Imagine that I just gave you a small amount of your favorite treat. This could be anything you choose, but you only get enough for THREE bites.

   You're hungry and that treat looks delicious! But before you eat it, I tell you that now you have two choices. I tell you that I'm about to leave the room, but I'll be back soon.
   You could eat your treat right now and enjoy it...
   OR
   You could wait till I come back in 15 minutes. If you do, I'll give you more of that treat.

   **WOULD YOU RATHER:**
   Gobble up your small treat right now...
   OR
   Wait 15 minutes so you can have twice as much of the treat?

   **WILL YOU:**
   Eat your treat right now...
   OR

Trade it with a friend so you can try a kind of treat you've never had before and eat it right now...
OR
Trade and wait?

**WOULD YOU RATHER:**
Find out that I was just trying to tease you and there is no double reward if you wait...
OR
Find out that this is a behaviour experiment, and what you tell us is something important about who you are AND possibly about your future? (See the note on page 86 for more about this scenario)

**10. WOULD YOU RATHER:**
Write a book that tells people how to do something...
OR
Write a fiction book (a book that tells a made-up story)?

Find out the book you wrote is going to be made into a TV series...
OR
Find out the book you wrote is going to be made into a movie?

Find out your favorite actor really wants to be in the TV series or movie made from your book...
OR

Be the person chosen to be the presenter or actor in the TV series or movie adapted from the book you wrote...

Receive a BIG award for the book you wrote, but only a little bit of money...
OR
Make a lot of money from sales of your book, but earn no awards?

## 11. WOULD YOU RATHER BE INVITED TO:

Sing on stage with Justin Bieber...
OR
Dance on stage with Beyoncé...
OR
Help your favourite actor write the next movie she or he will star in...
OR
Spend one day with your favorite celebrity (who are they and why did you choose them)?

Be a movie producer (they are the top boss of everything about making the movie)...
OR
Be the director of that movie (they tell the actors what to do)...
OR
Be the costume designer for the movie...
OR

Be the lead actor in that movie?

## 12. WOULD YOU RATHER:
Eat pizza...

OR

Spaghetti

OR

Salad?


Eat out at a very fancy restaurant...

OR

At a small restaurant, like a family pub or diner

OR

At your favorite fast-food restaurant

OR

Make a nice meal and eat it at home?


## 13. WOULD YOU RATHER:
Be given one really BIG gift for your next birthday (if so, what would it be?)...

OR

Receive 5 smaller gifts?


**14.** As an amateur anthropologist, you discover a cache of ancient gold coins. (Anthropologists study how people lived thousands of years ago.) Tell the story of how you made this amazing discovery.

How did you know where to look?

What tools did you use?

Who do you think might have buried these coins where you found them?

Why did they bury them?

What would you say to that person, if you could go back in time and meet them?

## 15. WHICH DO YOU LIKE THE MOST?

Baseball, basketball, football or soccer?

Tennis, badminton or volleyball?

Nerfball or floor hockey?

Skateboards, or bicycles?

Skates, or skis?

Scooters, or motorcycles?

Going on the bus, or going on the train?

Vacations that are close to home, or far away?

Sleeping in late, or getting up early?

## 16. WOULD YOU RATHER:

Be able to talk to any one type of animal...and what animal would it be?

OR

Be able to talk to all animals...

OR

Be able to listen to what all creatures say to each other and understand them perfectly? If this is your choice, you wouldn't be able to talk to them. Also, they wouldn't know that you can understand what they're saying to each other...

OR

Have all animals understand what you are saying AND thinking, but you don't know what they're thinking or saying.

Why?

## 17. WHICH IS YOUR FAVORITE?

Spring, or Fall (Autumn)?

Summer, or Winter?

Dogs, or Cats?

Vanilla, or chocolate?

Be early, be exactly on time, or be late?

Diving, or flying?

Superman, or Spiderman?

Wonder Woman, or Lois Lane?

Singing, or dancing?

Going to the beach, or going to a concert?

Visiting a museum, or visiting the zoo?

Red, green, blue, orange, yellow or purple?

Why?

## 18. WOULD YOU RATHER:

Be an actor...

OR

A comedian?

Be a banker...
OR
A farmer?

Wear glasses...
OR
Contact lenses?

**19.** You suddenly acquire ANY superpower that you can imagine. (Here are some ideas: perhaps you can see through walls, or fly like Superman, or you have a super-strength?)

What is your superpower?

How does it work?

How do you use your superpower?

**20.** You can be a character in ANY book you've ever read, or ANY TV show or movie you've ever seen.

Who will you be?

What will you do, as this character?

Why did you choose them?

**21.** You and a friend are getting together to do something special (this can be a good friend, or for a date).
**WOULD YOU RATHER:**
You plan where you'll go and what you'll do together...
OR
They plan everything...
OR
You share the planning for your time together?

There is a plan...
OR
There isn't any plan. You just hang out together and do whatever you both feel like doing?

**IF THERE IS A PLAN, WOULD YOU RATHER:**
Both people know what the plan is...
OR
One person is surprised?

**IF A SURPRISE, WOULD YOU RATHER:**
You are the one who's surprised...
OR
Your friend is the one who's surprised?

**22. WOULD YOU RATHER:**
Be a character in your favorite video game (who?)...
OR

Create a new video game character? (Who are they?)

Make a major change to your favorite video game (what is this change?)...
OR
Make a major change to the story in your favorite book?

Change a major rule in your favorite sport...
OR
Invent a new sport? (Tell us what it is and how you play it).

**23.** You are a successful photographer.
**WOULD YOU RATHER:**
Be a wedding photographer...
OR
Take all the student pictures during Photo Day at school?

Be a news photographer who takes pictures of disasters, like tropical storms...
OR
Takes pictures of everyday life?

Be a nature photographer, taking pictures of natural wonders, like sunrises and sunsets...
OR

Be a storm-chaser, taking pictures of hurricanes, lightning storms and volcanos erupting...
OR
Take pictures of your favourite wild birds or animals?

Be a fashion photographer, selling your photos to fashion magazines...
OR
You only take family photos...
OR
You only take photos of celebrities?

24. You've just invented a MAJOR improvement to computers. What is it?

    How does it work? Why will people want their computer to have this improvement?

25. You've just invented a new toy for children. What is it? (Your toy could be for babies, very young children, or kids of any age up to age 12).

    What does this toy look like?

    How does it work, if it has moving parts? Does it need a battery? Or could it run on solar power?

    Describe who will have fun playing with this toy, and why?

**26.** You've just thought up a MAJOR way to improve cars. What is it? What is so good about this improvement? Who does it help, and how?

How much will this improvement cost? Do you think that people who buy the cars will want to pay extra to get this improvement in their new car?

Give this improvement a name!

**27.** You wanted to go on a beach vacation, but your family (or friends) all want to go to the city.
**WOULD YOU RATHER:**
Skip the trip, telling them you'll just stay at home...
OR
Go on the trip, and maybe discover some new things you're interested in?

Visit a nearby city you've already been to and like...
OR
A city you've never been to before?

Visit a city in a very different part of your own country...
OR
Visit an exciting foreign city?

Visit a museum in that city...
OR
Go shopping?

**28.** You invent a way for people to travel to the centre of the earth and not get burnt to a crisp. Describe how this could be possible.

Now, you and some friends are taking this trip. Describe it!

**29. WOULD YOU RATHER:**
Meet a ghost and have a conversation with them...
OR
Be a ghost for one day and night?

Have a friendly ghost move into your room...
OR
Meet a scary ghost, just once?

Find a way to prove that ghosts really do exist...

OR
Find a way to prove that ghosts really do NOT exist?

Write an animated novel about a ghost...
OR
Paint a wall mural with a ghost in it?

Tell us the story in your novel or describe your wall mural.

**30.** You decide that you want to become a teacher.
**WOULD YOU RATHER:**
Teach very young children...
OR
kids who are ages 8 to 12...
OR
Teenagers...
OR
Adults...
OR
A mix of ages?

Teach science...
OR
History...
OR
Gym class?

Work in a big school...
OR

A small school, where everyone knows everyone else?

Teach music...
OR
Computer skills?

Coach the football team...
OR
The drama club?

**31.** You have convinced your school, or the company where you work, to switch to solar power.

How did you do it?

Describe what differences it will make to use solar power instead of electricity or a fossil fuel such as gas or oil.

**32.** Incredibly, you are asked to write an episode for your favorite animated TV show.

Using the characters from the show, create a story about them going on vacation together. You can have any of the characters go anywhere you want.

Who will go, and what will they do there?

Now, tell your story or write it!

**33.** YOU are invited to create a new reality show. It could be a talent show, a contest, a race, a game show, or any kind of reality show you choose.

The people who are the stars of this show could be kids, adults, families – it's your choice!

Your show will be on TV once a week and it will be 60 minutes long.

What is it about?

How are people chosen to be on the show?

Why will they want to be on the show?

What prizes will they be trying to win?

What will they have to do to win these prizes?

Why will people want to watch this show?

Give your new show a catchy name. Make it one people will be intrigued by and find easy to remember!

Pretend that you are trying to convince a major TV network (like Netflix or Showtime) to buy your new show and offer it to their viewers. What will you tell the people at the network that will convince them that they should invest in your new show?

Write a two-sentence blurb for your new show. A blurb briefly tells people what the show is about, who it's for, and why they'll love it.

You can use a blurb to describe any type of creative project.

Here's an example. It's the blurb for this book.

More Fun Jokes, Riddles and Scenarios for Happy Kids is a children's word game book for kids age 8 to 12. It has lots of funny jokes, what-if and would-you-rather scenarios and tricky riddle questions to entertain and delight kids plus hilarious cartoon illustrations.

Now it's your turn. Write the blurb for your new reality show!

**34.** You are given the opportunity to build the house of your dreams!

But to get the money you'll need to be able to create this dream home, you must promise to make it a GREEN home. This means your home will be as ecologically-friendly as possible. Ecologically-friendly means kind to our world and not creating more pollution or garbage.

Your home must be made entirely of recycled materials, like plastic water bottles, soda pop cans, glass bottles, or building materials taken from old buildings when they're torn down.

Describe what your dream house looks like and how you will build it out of recycled materials. Remember to tell us everything about how this house is Green. This means, all the special energy-saving features along with all the recycled materials used and how these were used.

Here are some questions to get you started:

**WOULD YOU RATHER:**
Convert a garage behind a city house into your dream home…
OR
Build a new house on a city lot?

Convert an old barn or abandoned store into a new home…
OR
Convert an old school or church into several apartments (flats) including one for you?

Build your house into the side of a hill, to save on heating costs…
OR

Put a flat roof on your house and make a roof garden?

Use solar panels for energy for your house...
OR
Use wind power for all your energy needs?

**35.** You are an explorer who discovers something that no one knew existed until you found it.

This might be a plant, an animal, a mineral, a lost city or civilization...OR?

What is it?

How did you find it?

Why will people want to know more about it?

When you announce your amazing discovery to the world, what will you say?

**36.** You are travelling in a very remote part of the world, where very few people ever go. Then, to your amazement, you meet a group of people who think THEY are the only people on earth, because they've never seen other people except themselves.

Who are these mysterious people?

Are they afraid of you?

They are ready to attack! Are you afraid of them?

Are they friendly? Curious?

How do they live?

How have they been hidden from everyone else for so long?

Now that you've found them, will you keep their secret? Or tell the world about them?

Why will you make this choice?

How could this change the way they live?

Do you think meeting them could change your life? If so, how?

**37.** What if, one day, you wake up to find out that now you have a different skin color than the one you were born with? How do you think this might change your life?

OR

You wake up one morning to find out you are suddenly a very different age than you are right now. You could be much younger, or much older. What age are you? How does this change your life?

OR

You wake up one morning to find out that one part of your body doesn't work any more the way it did. Doctors are mystified. While they try to figure out what's wrong, you need to live with this one part of your body not working the way you're used to.

Perhaps you have lost your hearing, or your sense of smell, or now your legs don't work. Or one arm doesn't work, including the hand you usually write with.

Your doctors are sure they can help you, but until they do: what ability did you lose and how does it change your life?

Tell this story or write it!

38. What would change in your life if you (or your family) didn't have a car? (If your family currently doesn't have a car, what would change in your life if you or your family got a car?)

How would you get to school, or work and everywhere else you want to go? Would you walk everywhere? Take a bus, or train, or monorail?

Get a ride with a friend?

Ride a bike, or a scooter?

If you already do some or all these things because your family doesn't have a car, would you stop doing them if you got a car?

What do you think our world be like without cars? How would people get to where they need to go?

**39.** Someone who is a close friend or family member is getting married. You are choosing a special gift to give them.
**WOULD YOU RATHER:**
Make their gift...
OR
Buy a gift?

Give them something they can use in their home...
OR
Give them something they can use on their honeymoon trip?

That they open the gift when you are visiting them before the wedding...
OR
Open their gifts when you aren't around?

What will your gift be, and why did you choose it? If you are making their gift, tell what it is and how you will create it.

If you are buying their gift, tell how you will earn the money to buy it and how you will shop for it.

40. Almost 200 years ago, Johannes Sax invented a new musical instrument.

Today, this instrument is played in thousands of orchestras and bands around the world. It's known as the saxophone.

Now it's your turn to invent a musical instrument!

What is it, what does it sound like and what does it look like?

What will it be called?

41. Choose ANY appliance in your home. An appliance is any machine that runs on energy and is used to solve a problem, like a stove (cooktop) to cook your food, a washer to clean your clothing or hair tongs to straighten your hair.

Some other appliances you might use are refrigerators, toasters, microwave ovens and hair dryers.

What change, or changes would you make to the appliance you've chosen to make it better?

How and why would it be better?

**42.** Invent a new type of snack food.

What does it look like?

Smell like?

Taste like?

Is it sweet? Salty? Crispy? Crunchy? Smooth?

Why will people want to buy it?

Give it a name.

Write the blurb for your new product that will be sent to managers for grocery stores, urging them to sell this new treat in the snacks sections of their stores.
Now, write an advertisement for your delicious new snack food! This could be an advertisement you might see online, in a magazine, on TV, or before they show the movie at a theatre.

**43.** Your family is moving abroad for two or three years.
**WOULD YOU RATHER:**
Go with them...
OR
Stay where you live now?

Is this a country that you've been to on vacation,
and really like...
OR
A place you've never been, but would love to go to?

Do you want to choose what country you go to...
OR
Do you want to be told what country your family is
going to?

Do you want to go to a country in Europe...
OR
South America...
OR
North America...
OR
Asia
OR
Africa
OR
Would you rather go to Australia?

44. You are asked to give some good advice for new
teachers who are going to teach your grade in
school or a class you are in now.

What will you recommend?

What can you tell them that will help them be
better teachers?

What can you tell them to improve the class or course they teach for future students like you?

**45.** You want to invite someone special to dinner, but you know you aren't a very good cook.
**WOULD YOU RATHER:**
Treat them to a restaurant meal…
OR
Try to make something anyways, maybe something simple like hot dogs or bacon and eggs or a salad…
OR
Buy a take-out (take-away) meal, then tell them you made it…
OR
Learn how to make one 'fancy' meal well so you can make it for your friend when they come to visit?

Should this meal be a picnic…
OR
A back-yard barbeque…
OR
A sit-down meal?

Will you make them a hot breakfast…
OR
A simple lunch…
OR
A special dinner?

**46.** You have a job. For this job, you are required to work 7 hours on 5 days every week. On each day that you work, you get two 15-minute breaks plus 20 minutes to eat a meal. AND you get to choose which days and which hours you will work.
**WOULD YOU RATHER:**
Work Monday to Friday and have every weekend off work...
OR
Always work on the weekends, but get any two week days off that you choose?

Always work daytime hours...
OR
Always work when it's dark out?

Work exactly the same hours every week...
OR
Work different hours each week?

Work longer hours in the winter (cold season) but have more time off in summer...
OR
Work more in summer and less in winter?

Start your workday at 8 a.m. ...
OR
Start your workday at 10 a.m.?

Choose your work hours...

OR
Be told what hours you are expected to work?

**47.** Your work must be exceptional, because you just got a raise, or a promotion!
**WOULD YOU RATHER:**
Get a raise, so you earn more money, but still do the same job...
OR
Get a promotion, meaning you get a better job, but you still make the same amount of money?

Teach other people how to get a raise, or a promotion...
OR
Take a course on how to get a raise or a promotion...
OR
Read a book about how to get a raise or a promotion, then try what it suggests doing?

Get BOTH a raise and a promotion, but you must spend two hours every day to get to work and home again...
OR
Start your own business, be your own boss and work in your home office?

Why?

**48.** You get a volunteer job. Its your chance to do something different and fun, learn new skills, meet new friends and give to an important cause helping people, animals or the environment.
**WOULD YOU RATHER:**
Volunteer to help protect the home of an endangered species, such as shore birds?
OR
Plant trees...
OR
Work with rescued cats, dogs and other pets, helping to care for them and help them find good new homes...
OR
Help out at a food bank or soup kitchen, helping homeless people?

Do your volunteer job inside, at a desk...
OR
Inside, but standing or walking around...
OR
Outside?
In a costume, because you are a guide at a historic attraction...
OR
In your own casual clothes?

**49.** You decide to get more exercise.
**WOULD YOU RATHER:**

Get up earlier every morning, so you can swim laps at the pool before you go to school or to work?

OR

Go for a run every evening...

OR

Work out with weights and exercise videos at home...

OR

Sign up for a class in aerobics that meets three times a week...

OR

Get a dog and take her for two brisk 30-minute walks every day?

**50.** You are planning what would be your favourite summer party and inviting your 10 closest friends. What sort of party will this be?
**WOULD YOU RATHER:**

Go rock-climbing or wall-climbing with your friends...

OR

Treat everyone to a restaurant dinner, followed by a play or a concert?

OR

Have a backyard barbeque, with a band and fireworks?

OR

Have a pool party?

**51.** As an amateur astronomer (they study stars, planets and everything in the universe beyond earth), you've discovered a new comet, star or planet. Now, you have the honour of naming it.

What did you discover?

What will it be called?

Why?

**52.** As an amateur geologist (they study rocks and how the earth was formed), you discover a new type of metal. It is somewhat like other metals we already know about and use, such as gold, silver, copper and lead. But it is also different in several important ways.

How is this new metal like other metals?

How is it different? What astonishing things can it do or be used for that metals we already have can't?

What will you name this new metal?

Describe it.

Write the blurb for this new metal you will send to other scientists.

## 53. WOULD YOU RATHER:

Be able to bake a cake…
OR
Make a pizza, from scratch?

Work in a store…
OR
Drive a truck?

Give a speech…
OR
Take an exam…
OR
Write an essay?

Paint a picture…
OR

Paint walls in your home?

**54. WOULD YOU RATHER:**
Own a crystal ball that allows you to always be able to tell the future for anyone, EXCEPT yourself...
OR
Know someone who has a crystal ball and knows how to use it, so you could always find out what would happen for you in the future...
OR
Never know what might happen in the future until it happens?

**55. WOULD YOU RATHER:**
Work for a long time, possibly years, knowing at the end you'd find a lost treasure...
OR
Search for treasure for years, not knowing what you'd find or even if you'd ever find anything of interest or value...
OR
Watch programs or read books about other people searching for lost treasures and what they find?

**56. WOULD YOU RATHER:**
Live on a farm and have lots of animals, including pets...
OR

Live in a city apartment, and only be able to have
very small pets like a cat or a gerbil...

OR

Not have any pets?

Why?

## 57. WOULD YOU RATHER:

Live in a large home that you share with many other
family members including your grandparents,
aunts, uncles and cousins...

OR

Live in a small house, with just your own family of
parents, brothers, sisters and pets?

## 58. WOULD YOU RATHER:

Be the tallest person you know...

OR

Be taller than you are now...

OR

Be exactly as tall as you are right now for all your
life...

OR

Be shorter than you are now?

Why?

## 59. WOULD YOU RATHER:

Own and work at a landscaping business...

OR

A dentists' office...

OR

A grocery store...

OR

A fashion boutique?

## 60. WOULD YOU RATHER:

Be a mechanic who fixes cars...

OR

Be the person who sells auto parts at the automotive store...

OR

Work at the factory where the auto parts are made?

Why?

## 61. WOULD YOU RATHER:

Be a player on a team playing your favourite sport...

OR

Be the captain of this sports team...

OR

Be the coach of this sports team?

## 62. WOULD YOU RATHER:

Drive the Batmobile...

OR

A solar-powered car in a solar car race...

OR

Have your own electric car to drive to school and everywhere else you want to go?

### 63. WOULD YOU RATHER:

Draw a treasure map…

OR

Be the person chosen to hide this treasure map…

OR

Be the person who finds the treasure map, but you can't understand what it says, because it's in code…

OR

The code-breaker who reveals what the map shows and helps to find the treasure?

### 64. WOULD YOU RATHER:

Design beautiful and functional furniture…

OR

Be the craftsperson who makes this furniture…

OR

Be the person who sells this furniture to people who want beautiful, comfortable homes?

### 65. WOULD YOU RATHER:

Buy that home, with all the furniture already in it…

OR

Buy the home, but choose your own furniture…

OR

Just rent the home, so that you can easily change your mind and live somewhere else, if you choose to?

**66. WOULD YOU RATHER:**

Just talk into your computer and it would write out the words for you, so you wouldn't need a keyboard...

OR

Have a computer that could read your mind, so you didn't have to type in the words and didn't have to speak them, either...

OR

Have exactly the computer you have right now, with the same keyboard?

**67. WOULD YOU RATHER:**

Have the family car you have now...

OR

Have a different car of your choice (what is it?)...

OR

Not own a car...

OR

Have a car that drives itself? All you need to do is sit back and enjoy the view!

**68.** You've decided to open a bakery and café, but you've noticed that the bakeries that have a theme are more prosperous than bakeries that don't. So, you'll need to choose what your speciality or theme is going to be.

**WOULD YOU RATHER:**

Open a bakery known for its incredible cupcakes...

OR

Stunning wedding cakes…
OR
It offers 37 types of pies…
OR
It makes beautiful breads and rolls, using heritage grains…
OR
Invent a new type of bakery. What will it sell, and why will your customers love it and keep coming back for more?

**69.** When you open your bakery café, you won't be able to do ALL the jobs there are.
**WOULD YOU RATHER:**
Be the baker? Remember, the baker will need to come in at 3 a.m. every morning to make the cookies, cupcakes, cakes or pies.
OR
Would you like to be the office person, who runs everything, orders the supplies and manages the staff…
OR
Would you rather be out front, selling the goodies and serving customers…
OR
Do you want to be the delivery person, taking your cakes or pies to other restaurants you also sell to?

**70.** Most people have one super-talent. Some have more than one. This could be a natural ability for sports, or music, or languages, or art, or any of dozens of other gifts they were lucky enough to be born with.

**WOULD YOU RATHER:**

Have a gift for languages, making it easy for you to quickly learn any language of your choice...

OR

Have a gift for sports, and what sport would you choose?

OR

Have a gift for music, so you can learn to play several instruments and any type of music, and what would these be?

OR

Have a gift for numbers – you can easily do math in your head...

OR

Have a gift for entertaining people, and what kind of entertainer would you be? Some ideas: would you be an actor, a singer, a dancer, a magician? Or possibly a storyteller, a comedian or a performer in a circus?

**71.** Think about your one super-talent.

**WOULD YOU RATHER:**

Find out what it is when you are very young, so that part of your childhood is spent taking lessons and practicing skills to develop your talent...

OR

Not find out about your super-talent until you are a young adult...

OR

Know about your talent, but not have the opportunity to develop it until you are an older adult...

OR

Would you know about your talent, but prefer not to develop it with lessons and practice so that you have more time for your other interests and responsibilities?

**72.** HRH Prince Harry is coming to visit your school!
**WOULD YOU RATHER:**

Be chosen to be one of the students who greets him...

OR

Be the person invited to give him a tour of your school...

OR

Be one of the people chosen to have lunch with him?

## How to Create Your Own Limericks

Did you spot the limericks in this book?

Limericks are short, funny and usually very silly poems.

Here is one you might already have heard because it's the world's most famous limerick:

There was an old man with a beard
Who said, "It is just as I feared!
Two owls and a hen,
a lark and a wren
have all built their nests in my beard!"

This limerick was written more than 170 years ago. This limerick is included in **The Book of Nonsense** by Edward Lear, a book for children published in 1846.] He wasn't the first person to write limericks, but his limericks became very popular. People still enjoy them today so much that Mr. Lear's birthday, May 12, is National Limerick Day in many nations, including his own, Great Britain.

Here's what all limericks have:
- Limericks always have 5 lines. Lines 1, 2 and 5 rhyme. Lines 3 and 4 rhyme with each other.

- Lines 1, 2 and 5 are a bit longer than lines 3 and 4.
- The first line often ends with the name of a person or a place.
- The last line is funny.

Go back and read Edward Lear's limerick about the old man and you'll see that his limerick has all these things.

Limericks also have a bouncy rhythm, so when you read them out loud they sound like this:

"da DUM da da DUM da da DUM,
da DUM da da DUM da da DUM.
da DUM da da DUM,
da DUM da da DUM,
da DUM da da DUM da da DUM!"

Now that you know these limerick writing secrets, are you ready to try writing your own limericks?

Start with line 1. Choose a person or a place and write it. Your first line could be "There was a young girl from Toronto," or "There was a strange fellow from Chicago," or "There was a striped horse named York," or anything you choose!

Now, think of lots of words that rhyme with the last word in your line 1. You might look at a rhyming dictionary for help. Write down all your rhyming words, choose 2, and write your limerick's line 2 and line 5.

Now choose 2 other rhyming words and fill in line 3 and line 4.

Read your limerick out loud to be sure it has the right rhythm (the da DUMs).

You'll need to make changes to make your limerick work and be even funnier.

Limericks are tricky – you need to get the rhyme, the rhythm and the length just right as well as the joke at the end. Like all writing, it takes some practice!

Have fun writing your limericks and sharing them with family and friends!

*In this book, we've shared some fun times*
*with lots of jokes, riddles and rhymes.*
*You've also told stories,*
*of fortune, fame, success and glory.*

*There were choices, too*
*about what you might do*
*with your life, well lived.*
*What you'll get; what you'll give.*

*Go back through this book any time*
*you're in need of a smile, a laugh or a rhyme.*
*Your answers might change,*
*or you could re-arrange*

*what you think about you*
*and what you can do*
*to light up your life.*
*To reduce stress or strife.*

*To bring joy to yourself and others;*
*friends, family, sisters, brothers.*
*So now comes the time,*
*To end this book, and this rhyme.*

*Farewell and adieu,*
*fond best wishes to you!*

Myles O'Smiles

Scenario #9 on page 43 is based on a real science study, called The Marshmallow Experiment, done with children at Stanford University in United States by psychologist Walter Mischel.

Children were offered one small marshmallow, pretzel, candy or cookie that they could eat right away, or they could wait to eat later. If they waited 15 minutes, they'd get twice as much of the treat for their reward.

A follow-up study several years later found that children who were able to wait did better in school and their lives were better in other ways. Find out more at https://www.ncbi.nlm.nih.gov/pubmed/5010404 and Journal of Personality and Social Psychology. 16 (2): 329–337.

That's all, Kids!

THANKS for reading!

## About the Author

Myles O'Smiles is a former teacher and current book writer who believes that the very best way to learn something is when you enjoy it.

His mission is to make kids laugh while they learn!

He lives with his family in a treehouse, where he enjoys anything that's silly, taking long elderberry tea breaks, gazing out at the stars and thinking up new word game and activity books for kids.

Here are all the books he's written, so far:

- Fun Jokes for Funny Kids
- Clever Scenarios for Clever Kids
- Awesome Riddles for Awesome Kids
- More Fun Jokes, Riddles and Scenarios for Happy Kids

If you haven't read all the Myles O'Smiles books yet, you can find them here:

### www.mylesosmiles.com

You can also write to Myles and tell him your favorite joke!

# www.MylesOSmiles.com

CPSIA information can be obtained
at www.ICGtesting.com
Printed in the USA
FSHW010924081218
54332FS